T0380823

GOOD FRUIT

Preparing the Soil of Your Small Family Business
to Yield Good Fruit

Jacqueline Carlisle

AuthorHouse™
1663 Liberty Drive
Bloomington, IN 47403
www.authorhouse.com
Phone: 833-262-8899

Because of the dynamic nature of the Internet, any web addresses or links contained in this book may have changed since publication and may no longer be valid. The views expressed in this work are solely those of the author and do not necessarily reflect the views of the publisher, and the publisher hereby disclaims any responsibility for them.

This book is printed on acid-free paper.

ISBN: 978-1-6655-1030-1 (sc)
ISBN: 978-1-6655-1031-8 (e)

Library of Congress Control Number: 2020924276

Print information available on the last page.

Published by AuthorHouse 12/28/2020

authorHOUSE®

Contents

Dedication

This book is dedicated to Paul Edward Chambers, Justin Angrand and Darian Ashley, My Inspirations.

Preface

SEE SOMETHING; SAY SOMETHING

11 And have no fellowship with the unfruitful works of darkness, but rather expose them. 12 For it is shameful even to speak of those things which are done by them in secret. 13 But all things that are exposed are made manifest by the light, for whatever makes manifest is light.
- Ephesians 5:11-13 (NKJV)

I never planned to write this book. I never expected to be an author nor thought I had a story to tell. After all, I figured there were already so many books – what more needed to be said?

I began researching how to improve a family business when my family's enterprise faced challenges that were beyond my understanding. I look at life through the lens of identifying problems and providing solutions, but this did not happen in our business, nor did it happen in our family.

I was confused. I couldn't understand how small issues became large, why getting anything done was difficult, and why nothing was ever resolved, just swept under the rug.

As I began to read books and articles about how family businesses *should* operate and the inherent problems in some family businesses, I began to gain a deeper understanding. I had been focusing on the effects, not the causes.

This book contains several many Scripture references. I have come to the conclusion that the problems many family businesses face are rooted not only in the physical realm, but the spiritual realm as well. Because I have come to the conclusion the root of what occurs in struggling family businesses is not merely physical, but spiritual. As Ephesians 6:12 states,

"For our struggle is not against flesh and blood, but against the rulers, against the authorities, against the powers of this dark world and against the spiritual forces of evil in the heavenly realms" (NIV).

I implore readers to consider the book from this perspective. This book is not about people nor personalities: it is about that which is operating within the heart (spirit) and is manifested into actions seen and experienced by others. Please do not allow blind protection of family roles to cloud the larger picture. The lens of my larger picture is to remove the film which may cloud judgement so that we may see the fruit of the spirit displayed in and flourishing through every individual in your family business. Doing this will benefit the individual, the family, the business and the community for the glory of God.

The Fruit of the Spirit as shared in Galatians 5:22-23, reads "But the fruit of the Spirit is love, joy, peace, forbearance, kindness, goodness, faithfulness, [23] gentleness and self-control. Against such things there is no law" (NIV).

Therefore, a spiritual and biblical worldview is important to examine this work of my heart to yours.

Nothing can be resolved by only dealing with outward symptoms. I never even thought about the underlying causes; however, they were revealed in therapy and contextualized in ministerial school. It was then that I first understood what it meant to function in dysfunction.

In the end, a collection of ideas changed the way I viewed my family's business. These ideas allowed me to better understand what our entity should and could be, and most importantly, they provided the tools I needed to critically and courageously examine our business and family dynamic. Discovering those ideas was transformative, and the process of pulling them together evolved into writing this book.

I wanted more people to experience these concepts so that they too might have the opportunity to make impactful change in their businesses and lives.

All that said, this book is more of a work of art than science. I am no expert in business planning, formation, or organizational development, nor a professional in psychology or human behavior. I am a person who has always believed that systems can operate to the best of their potential when people authentically work together, respect one another, and build quality relationships founded on kindness, honesty, transparency, and universal growth.

I hope this book will help others see where they may be wrapping their lives around a business that looks fine on the surface, but in reality, may not be serving them or their families. I'd like to help others learn to identify these often hidden challenges, to heal if possible and to be empowered to disengage if achieving the goal of flourishing is not possible.

Through my personal struggles, I have learned that allowing deep-seated challenges to go unchecked in a family business steals creativity, wastes resources, and is inherently crippling. Attempting to thrive rather than addressing these challenges is the wrong response. Unhealthy patterns must be disrupted, not tolerated. They can be eradicated by eliminating co-dependence; they cannot persist without willing participants.

This book aims to aid others in identifying, acknowledging and addressing deep-seated challenges so that they may live productive and empowering lives built on clarity and in the company of others who seek the same. I am hopeful that others can relate to my experience and gain clarity to see solutions that offer a way forward in their journeys.

> **17** *Even so, every good tree bears good fruit, but a bad tree bears bad fruit.*
> *- Matthew 7:17 (NKJV)*

Introduction

"To solve our most difficult problems, we must radically change our thinking."
- Stephen Covey

5 Trust in the Lord with all your heart,
And lean not on your own understanding;
6 In all your ways acknowledge Him,
And He shall direct your paths.
- Proverbs 3:5-6 (NKJV)

I want to give family-owned businesses the best resource to guide their success. I'd also like to give them the resource I wish was available years ago to guide my insights and decisions – nuggets of information to address problems I was not aware existed until they came unavoidably to the surface based on my research.

This book is a result of my labor in a family business for over 25 years and my association with many others who work in family businesses. Through these experiences, I have gained valuable insight into the risks these businesses face in trying to survive while protecting their family units.

Change is the fundamental goal of this book and it is embedded in how family businesses operate. I want to help facilitate this change by uncovering critical and latent issues impacting family businesses.

Experiencing and observing the challenges and strife within my family's business, I often wondered, "why?" For a very long time, I could not figure out the root of the problem until I learned that the key to understanding the difficulty was becoming aware of the underlying issues. The issues are multifaceted and not obvious. This conclusion led me to an "aha" moment.

Nothing can be resolved if you do not first know what is broken.

This book offers vital information that will allow those participating in a family business to evaluate their issues in a new dimension.

Being transparent and sharing the truth regarding the family business is a major obstacle, and the reason is fear: fear of exposing flaws, fear of what others will think, fear of seeming disloyal when others within the business are resistant to sharing information outside of the family unit. However, I believe that transparency leads to understanding, and understanding can lead to positive change.

Seventy-five percent of family-owned businesses do not survive past the first generation. The rate of failure is extremely high, despite the best motivations and intentions of the participants. The family business often lacks the leadership, accountability, and structural foundations of traditional business models.

I discovered that many people are not willing to publicly share the challenges they face in family business. Instead, they complain privately with close friends and family members. But, these people cannot provide solutions if the underlying causes of those challenges are not identified.

I want to share what I have learned by shedding light on common issues and providing practical guidance to encourage change where needed – change that will lead to a successful business and harmonious family.

I have witnessed the quiet disintegration of many family businesses and have discovered the patterns that contributed to their downfalls. Patterns that are not serving the family or the business must be disrupted if change is to occur.

Realizing the importance of the following elements is critical for sustainable growth and expansion:

- Inspirational leadership
- Effective commumication
- Respect
- Trustfulness
- Defined roles/responsibilities
- Rewards and appreciation
- Transparency
- Vision
- Accountability
- Personal and professional goals
- Equitable financial distribution
- Planning

The unique dynamics of family businesses mean they often forgo typical business structure, especially in these key areas. Since the family business model is unique, although not uncommon, it typically does not benefit from the traditional organizational structure and levels of accountability of non-family-owned businesses. Therefore, there is an inherent inability to organically craft internal solutions designed to support the goals of the business.

When these systemic issues are not embraced or addressed, the financial, physiological, and emotional price paid by the business and individuals is often immense.

I hope this book helps your business succeed while solidifying your strong family bonds!

"When everything seems to be going against you, remember that the airplane takes off against the wind, not with it."

- Henry Ford

Chapter 1

LACK OF CLEAR VISION AND STRATEGIC PLANNING

"Good business leaders create a vision, articulate the vision, passionately own the vision, and relentlessly drive it to completion."

- Jack Welch

Scripture Reference

2 Then the Lord answered me and said:
"Write the vision
And make it plain on tablets,
That he may run who reads it.
3 For the vision is yet for an appointed time;
But at the end it will speak, and it will not lie.
Though it tarries, wait for it;
Because it will surely come,
It will not tarry.

- Habakkuk 2:2-3 (NKJV)

T here are two keys to planning: *The first key is to clarify direction to describe what the business is or what it intends to be over time.* Clarifying the purpose and direction of your business allows you, and most importantly, others who support the business, to understand what needs to be done to move the enterprise forward. *The second key is to communicate the vision, which should include a code of ethics or key principles on which the business is founded.*

As businesses evolve and adapt over time, factoring future growth and direction into the business plan can help you effectively plan for changes in the market, growing or slowing trends, and new innovations or directions to take as the company grows.

Lack of a clearly developed and effectively communicated vision cripples the ability to gain sustainable long-term support from family and non-family employees, partners, customers, and other stakeholders.

We often hear that the basis of any good business plan is a firmly established vision and mission. Yet, more often than not, family-owned businesses neglect to develop a vision or mission statement. This is usually because the founders fail to see the necessity of sharing their vision with the outside world and do not understand the importance of planning for the internal benefit and longevity of the operation.

However, family-owned businesses can greatly benefit from developing such statements and dedicating time to their development and execution. A strong and effectively communicated vision will be infectious, stimulating, and attractive to others, and it will motivate all to achieve business goals and aspirations. *People rally around leaders with a compelling vision and a clear sense of purpose.* That is why creating a strong vision is one of the essential functions a business can perform.

For this book, we are describing the overall vision of the organization – *as an evolving manifestation of the founders'/owners' intention for the business that allows others to align with them in support of their own individual goals and objectives.*

A vision statement compels people to do something, change something, and become something. It is this drive that can transform a business into a strong, vibrant, and rewarding opportunity for everyone who comes into contact with it. Having an articulated vision statement supersedes individual goals and personalities while allowing for transparency in decision making. This helps to circumvent misunderstandings and guide organizational direction.

Another important function of a clearly defined vision and mission statement is attracting and retaining team members. The vision should be shared with the family, job candidates, or desired partners to help convince them of the potential for the business and persuade them to join the team.

A strong vision can create the requisite energy and drive to push and pull the business forward. An articulated vision is invaluable because it is *a realistic snapshot of the company in the future as well as a beacon of inspiration and the framework for strategic planning.*

The family-owned business can reap the benefits of a strong vision by *making it the centerpiece of the company's core values* and its purpose, describing the perspective for the business in the future, and then clearly communicating and living the vision at every opportunity. Again, the vision should be the evolving manifestation of the founder's intention for the business.

> *"The vision is really about empowering workers, giving them all the information about what is going on so they can do a lot more than they have done in the past."*
> - Bill Gates

Once a vision is created, organizations are more dynamically led. A genuinely great vision will come to life in the everyday actions and behavior of the family-owned business. It becomes the heartbeat of the organization's culture.

Vision statements give direction for the stakeholder's behavior and *provide a source of inspiration.* Furthermore, the vision can be a checkpoint for the viability of decisions made within the business. Far too often, participants in a family-owned business make decisions that are not aligned with any communicated vision and, therefore, those decisions may seem directionless to those charged with the execution of tasks. This results in a great deal of confusion.

The lack of built-in accountability to staff, family members, and others by the business founders/ owners can be a major issue impacting the viability of a family-owned business. A clear and articulated vision helps to build in a level of accountability, as all are accountable to the vision, and not only to a person. If the vision is not clear or actions are not in alignment with the vision, employees are likely to question the rationale of the leader's decisions and, more importantly, determine if the company's vision aligns with their own.

In most cases, a spouse or parent heads the business, and these personal, emotionally-charged relationship roles are brought into the business. Where there is no built-in accountability, some can behave irresponsibly. However, any irresponsibility impacts everyone. Therefore, to bridge this gap, the vision is essential for guiding the organization and organizational roles.

A business should have one, clear vision that all ascribe to and commit to reach. The development of this vision should be a collaborative effort that becomes the guiding force behind every decision made within the company. When the vision is clear, all members are focused on the same objectives and have confidence in the direction of the leader and the business.

A clear vision helps keep all parties informed as priorities shift within the business. Shifts may happen for many reasons in family-owned businesses, but at times, unilateral decisions imposed upon others may not necessarily be in the best interest of the entity. This can contribute to members deciding to leave the business when the decision making is not consistent with the vision.

The vision should be shared with all staff, clients, and customers. In addition, a training curriculum should be developed to introduce and communicate the vision to all staff, board members, and family members involved, as well as to support ongoing reinforcement.

This unified vision helps attract the right staff and serves as a foundation for an enhanced organizational culture. A unified vision that is well defined and articulated is important. Family members in leadership positions may assume that they understand what is best for all or that everyone intuitively understands an unspoken reason for the existence of the business or business-related decisions. Such assumptions, of course, can be unintentionally misleading.

Family members employed in the business should know the vision, be kept apprised of any changes to it, and have a say in the direction of the vision if they are expected to help develop it.

The development of a unified vision minimizes resistance to organizational direction. If the vision comes into conflict with actions, family members can judiciously identify actions or activities that are not in alignment with the agreed upon vision.

All stakeholders need to understand the common goals and assumptions upon which the business functions. What may be paramount to one person may not be as important to other family members employed in the business. For example, one family member may want a steady path for the business to support their personal livelihood and stability. However, another may want to grow and challenge their skills within the business, and then encounter resistance because their desired growth is outside the "status quo" of the organization.

A common vision will help all participants decide if joining or continuing in a family business is right for them and their long-term plans, both personally and professionally. Also, having a vision increases the influence of everyone involved, affording everyone the opportunity to clearly understand and impact the direction of the organization. Moreover, if there is a change in direction, a defined vision allows questions to be raised regarding why the vision was changed.

A clearly defined vision also decreases unilateral decision-making, helping to diminish confusion, empowering everyone involved, and allowing for absolute transparency that may not exist because of the design of many family-owned businesses. Furthermore, lack of a defined vision can communicate a negative message to anyone joining the business, one that suggests the business is directionless, not collaborative and can suffer from miscommunication and impaired growth.

The vision should be communicated consistently, both internally and externally, and all business operations and decisions made within the business should align with the vision. This is why it is important for the vision to be written, communicated, and clearly defined.

Often, there is no explicit vision, and the founder may be reluctant to share the implied vision. They may not have one, other than survival, but it is a necessary component for legacy building and cannot be forgone. Typically, the founder of the company is entrepreneurial in spirit and functions as the sole owner. In most cases, a founder relies upon a spouse or children to assist in running the business. Sometimes, when family members join in the business operations compulsorily due to a familial obligation, they are just assigned duties and do not have an effective voice. Frequently, family participation in the business comes at the expense of other opportunities for growth outside of the family-owned business. Therefore, when family members contribute to and support the growth of the business, they believe they will have some meaningful level of participation in charting the course of the entity.

If there is no explicit vision, it can be challenging to know how or where to focus efforts or align opportunities for growth. For example, is the goal of the business to stay small, or to grow? How is this calculated? How are potential employees vetted for positions: nepotism or qualifications? These are some of the questions that can be answered more readily if the business has a clearly defined vision.

In summary, a good vision:

- Identifies direction and purpose
- Builds loyalty through involvement
- Sets standards of excellence that reflect great ideas and a sense of integrity
- Is persuasive and credible
- Inspires enthusiasm and encourages commitment
- Is well articulated and easily understood
- Is ambitious and calls for a shared commitment
- Challenges and inspires people to align their energies in a common direction
- Fits with the unique culture and values of the business
- Results in efficiency and productivity
- Reflects the company's unique strengths

Some businesses state their vision as a mission statement, which "ideally serves to encapsulate the philosophy and expectations of a business and its owners," according to Scott E. Friedman in *The Successful Family Business.* Another vital component in communicating the vision is the development of a strategic plan based on the vision.

It is also helpful to support the vision with a strategic plan to gain the support of the staff. A strategic plan should be *visionary, conceptual, and directional.* It is a document used to communicate the organization's goals, the actions needed to achieve those goals and all the other critical elements developed during the planning exercise. A sound plan should:

- Serve as a framework for decisions or securing support and approval
- Provide a basis for more detailed planning
- Explain the business to inform, motivate, and involve others
- Assist in benchmarking and performance monitoring
- Stimulate change and become a building block for the next plan

As Scott E. Friedman notes, "a strategic plan instills a level of confidence among family members that their investment remains a good one; failure to develop and share such a plan may create the impression, deserved or not, that the business is much like a ship without a rudder and decisions are being made on an ad hoc basis instead of on the basis of a sensible long-term vision."

"Where there is no vision, there is no hope."

- G.W. Carver

Chapter 2

LACK OF SUPPORT STRUCTURES

"When your values are clear to you, making decisions becomes easier."
- Roy E. Disney

Scripture Reference

Unless the Lord builds the house,
They labor in vain who build it;
Unless the Lord guards the city,
The watchman stays awake in vain.

- Psalm 127:1 (NKJV)

According to *Family Business Successes and Failures* by Joachim Schwass, the objective is to build and manage a culture that benefits both the family and the business. This requires a code of conduct (or list of principles), that is carefully communicated.

The most successful family businesses understand the need for and have invested in support structures. A code of conduct, list of principles, family charter, and effective communication protocols can provide such support.

It is beautiful when family businesses work well together. However, it may be surprising that some family-owned businesses are plagued by steady drumbeats of disrespect, gossip, backbiting, and scapegoating. Since the subject of this book is how we can overcome barriers to success, it highlights areas of concern, explaining what they can look like so that we can identify the fault lines and apply solutions. Unfortunately, some of the debilitating behaviors that cause family breakdowns are brought into the business. The added pressure of interacting with people outside the family and business relationships creates further hardship if these outside relationships do not adhere to the business' family code of conduct or basic principles. A family code of conduct or basic guiding principles are critical vision supporting tools.

As outlined in *The Successful Family Business* by Scott E. Friedman, "to formalize a code of conduct establishes certain rules for behavior within a family business to ensure that a minimum level of courtesy and common decency exists within the business."

Friedman continues, "in our research, we have come across non-family CEOs who have praised family members working in the business by saying, 'they are more committed, they work harder, and they keep the family values alive and meaningful.' The family members who are passive owners are educated as responsible owners who have both rights and responsibilities. This seems to work best when they feel proud to be ambassadors for their family business.

According to Friedman, another effective tool is the creation of a family charter. A family charter is "created with the need to establish specific guidelines and rules that govern the interrelationships between family members with each other and the family business." A charter can be used to regulate such relationships and has been thought of as a sort of constitution for the family business.

Effective Systems

Imagine a set of scales with "staff/people" on one side and "systems" on the other, balancing one another. They are the two important elements that must be prioritized equally in the cycle to keep the business running. When both the people and the systems are equally strong, a family business owner can be confident that his or her business will be operating at a high level of effectiveness.

At any given time, the "scale" may be a bit out of balance. But if the two are consistently out of whack to the point that one is regularly strong and the other weak, you're headed for trouble. Great people working with poorly designed systems usually leads to burn out, or worse still, a situation in which the business fails to deliver so often that it gradually goes under despite everyone's best efforts to keep it afloat. In contrast, great systems without good people become hollow; they make for nice looking structures but create cultures in which people follow the rules so religiously that they make silly mistakes.

"Always treat your employees exactly as you want them to treat your best customers."
- Stephen Covey

Communication

A family-owned business' pattern of communication can be reflective of an offshoot of the family's communication patterns, which may not serve the business environment.

Clear communication is imperative. Family members generally have roles they play outside of the business, and each member has perceptions about the other players. Individuals may build alliances with other employees as they share their perspectives with others in the business.

The solution is to keep business and family discussions separate. Regardless of the personal relationships between team members, team members should act respectfully and professionally within the context of "work." Then, the "work" voice becomes a constructive critique rather than a personal attack.

In a family-operated business, the same communication trends that occur in the family structure often get transferred to the business, and this is another reason why many family-owned businesses fail to thrive. When effective communication is lacking in the household structure, lack will likely be reflected in the business' communications. However, when this failure of accountability invades business communications, it is the success of the business and the investments by individual family members that get incapacitated. This is one of the primary reasons many second-generation members decide to leave the business.

Everyone has heard the saying "communication is vital." Unfortunately, most people think that the saying applies only to others and that they may be communicating well. What really matters is how the information is received. In fact, that is the hallmark and true confirmation of effective communication. *Too often, we are quick to blame others for their perceived lack of understanding when it is always the responsibility of the sender to convey the meaning of their own message.*

Communication is essential for maintaining a productive workplace. By understanding the effects of negative communication in the workplace, you can develop policies that help to decrease the problem and encourage positive change.

According to Shannon and Weaver's model of communication, which they developed in 1948, "communication is the process of exchanging information, which could be conveyed as words, vocal tone, and body language. Studies have shown that words account for 7 percent of the information communicated. Vocal tone accounts for 55 percent and body language for 38 percent. Team members must know about these forms of communication and use them to communicate effectively."

Ineffective communication within a family-operated business can devolve into negative communication, including rumors, misinformation, misinterpretation, and incomplete information. While these elements may be purposely initiated, they often occur without any malicious intent, such as unknowingly relaying incomplete information.

Ineffective communication can cascade into several undesirable outcomes: misunderstandings, the withholding of information or input, inadequate feedback, and lack of innovation because new ideas are not welcomed.

If you speak with someone and they are confused, tired of the conversation, and just want the conversation to end, then you can be 100 percent certain the communication is not effective and the business will suffer.

With clear communication, all parties walk away understanding the issue at hand and how it can be addressed. At times, this does not occur in family-operated businesses.

I will go over a few communication styles and how they impede the success of a family business.

Broadcasting is a style of mostly one-way communication designed to raise awareness and encourage engagement. However, it can be used negatively to suppress change and growth, to maintain a status quo, and to prevent the emergence of innovative ideas and thought processes, which ultimately can debilitate the business.

Some can actually benefit from murky, obscure, and confusing engagements. Though this is more of a personality issue, it cannot be ignored as it can help others understand why there may never be a resolution of issues. The goal of many who benefit from this type of communication is not to resolve an issue. Rather, it is to prove their point or gain some perceived leverage. That is why conversations with this type of individual often lead nowhere. It is helpful in a family-operated business to understand this concept so that it may be appropriately identified and addressed.

Identifying ineffective communication styles as a barrier empowers members of the family-operated business to decide whether issues can be resolved. The remedy is to take a proactive approach and design an internal communication system with clear guidelines that support effective communication. Assuming transparency is the goal, there should be no resistance to improving this process. If there is resistance, this is yet another sign of the disserving culture of the family-operated business and can explain the resultant by-products of an ineffective communication system.

Often, the issue of identifying ineffective communication patterns is challenging because of resistance to change and refusal to accept that the communication system is inherently flawed. However, many family-owned businesses not only wish to survive, but thrive, and therefore, they are open to successful strategies that will support them in doing so. They are not defensive when confronted with issues and solutions; they are not intimidated by change. In fact, they fully understand that change can lead to unbridled growth.

Key Elements of Effective Communication Systems

Weekly Meetings

It is critical for business owners to consistently stay engaged with all staff in a way that allows for transparency, trust, and confidence building within the team. Often, family members have unofficial communications regarding the business outside of working hours, and all too frequently, this information may not be carried over to non-family staff or family members not present.

That sort of informal communication is, therefore, counterproductive. The solution is to establish a weekly meeting schedule for all staff with a prescribed agenda template. This will also decrease the need for family members to dive into business-related conversations during non-business gatherings. This is important because the infringement of business communications during non-business activities can create unnecessary stress and can be a boundary breach for those not interested in engaging in business-related conversation.

Transparency

It is vital to communicate clearly and transparently with staff and to avoid excluding anyone. Establish and adhere to rules regarding communication. Tone is very important, as it creates an environment in which people feel free to share their opinions openly, without being challenged or feeling threatened.

Transparency is crucial, as too often, the lines of communication can be fragmented. This leaves room for miscommunication and provides an opportunity for skeptics to drive a wedge between workplace staff. This can occur because there are people within the business who harbor personal insecurities, and their mode of operation is generally to promote confusion and division to meet their individual needs.

Again, the needs of the business can be superseded by an individual's personal needs, and this occurs easily when the business lacks effective, established, and transparent communication processes. When these systems are in place, they promote individual accountability, which can aid in preventing workplace gossip from effectively scapegoating other staff members.

If the mission of a family-owned business is to "provide the best computer service experience," then any conversation that does not contribute to the focus on providing the best computer service experience is unnecessary. When people engage in conversations or projects that do not promote this core vision, then the conversation or projects should be abandoned.

How is this determined? Simply ask, "how does this conversation fulfill the organization's vision of providing the best computer service experience?" If the participant cannot answer this question in 30 seconds or less, then the conversation is probably not in alignment with the vision, and the communication is perhaps ineffective and unproductive.

This focus on the core mission or vision forces all parties in a conversation to be accountable for what they say in a transparent way. So, the dialogue can always be steered into a meaningful conversation. This also helps manage unreasonable staff members – they'll know this question will be asked if they bring up topics that are contrary to the vision. In turn, they will become more accountable for the conversations they start, as the foundation has already been laid for intervention should they venture off-topic. This also empowers lower-level staff so that they are not forced to listen to unproductive opinions from other staff members.

To help family-owned businesses understand the four basic communication styles, descriptions and ramifications of each style are listed below. Being aware of styles employed by participants at any given time can assist in identifying where some issues may need to be addressed.

Most importantly, being aware of the negative implications of divergent communication styles can help lead to culture change, which will be imperative to successful growth, sustainability, enticing quality staff, and fostering quality working relationships, both internally and externally. The assertive is the most beneficial and productive communication style for family-owned businesses.

An understanding of the various communication styles can provide some insight into how we can be more responsible for engaging in effective communication. Identifying the different communication styles and inherent impacts within the family business can shed light on potential concerns that must be addressed within the enterprise.

Poor communication and decreased productivity go hand-in-hand. Whether poor communication is vertical (from manager to employee) or horizontal (employee to employee), a business' goal of high productivity can be undermined by ineffective communication. It is important to be concise with directives.

The Four Communication Styles

> *1 A soft answer turns away wrath, but a harsh word stirs up anger.*
> *2 The tongue of the wise uses knowledge rightly, but*
> *the mouth of fools pours forth foolishness.*
> *Proverbs 15:1-2 (NKJV)*

As noted by Carl Benedict on the website serenityonlinetherapy.com, there are four main communication styles – each is described below. I have also noted each style's impact on business.

Passive communication is a style in which individuals have developed a pattern of avoiding expressing their opinions or feelings, protecting their rights, or identifying and meeting their own needs.

The impact of a pattern of passive communication is that these individuals:

- often feel anxious because life seems out of their control
- often feel depressed because they feel stuck and hopeless
- often feel resentful (unknowingly) because their needs are not being met
- often feel confused because they ignore their own feelings
- are unable to mature because real issues are never addressed

Aggressive communication is a style in which individuals express their feelings and opinions and advocate for their needs in a way that violates the rights of others. Thus, aggressive communicators are verbally or physically abusive.

The impact of a pattern of aggressive communication is that these individuals:

- become alienated from others
- alienate others
- generate fear and hatred in others
- always blame others instead of owning their issues, and are unable to mature

Passive-aggressive communication is a style in which individuals appear passive on the surface but are really acting out anger in a subtle, indirect, or behind-the-scenes way.

The impact of a pattern of passive-aggressive communication is that these individuals:

- become alienated from those around them
- remain stuck in a position of powerlessness
- discharge resentment while real issues are never addressed so they cannot mature

Assertive communication is a style in which individuals clearly state their opinions and feelings, and firmly advocate for their rights and needs without violating the rights of others.

The impact of a pattern of assertive communication is that these individuals:

- feel connected to others
- feel in control of their lives
- can mature because they address issues and problems as they arise
- create a respectful environment for others to grow and mature

Consequences of Ineffective Communication and How This Hinders the Family Business

19 [a] So then, my beloved brethren, let every man be
swift to hear, slow to speak, slow to wrath;

- James 1:19 (NKJV)

According to George N. Root III in his smallbusiness.chron.com blog, low morale is a result of negative communication patterns. Habitual negative communication may increase stress and reduce staff confidence in the business. Demoralized employees may lack enthusiasm. Eventually, employees devalue their employer's business and may seek employment elsewhere.

Collaboration and positive, open communication promote skills beneficial to a healthy work environment: creativity, inspiration, and productivity. Business communication skills impact the motivation of employees. Projects are completed accurately and efficiently with proper communication. Employees feel comfortable asking clarifying questions without fear of ridicule or repercussions. *Confidence becomes a result of positive communication.*

Organizational structure is strongly affected by negative communication. Individuals or departments within an organization lose the ability to function interdependently when negative communication is the norm. This breakdown in organizational structure also leads to decreased productivity. The quickest way to increase morale is to put an immediate stop to negative communication.

Lower efficiency is also a result of unclear communication processes. Indirect email messages, inefficient meetings, and sloppy presentations can reduce a company's workflow. Projects involving multiple individuals or departments in which there is a lack of direct communication also decreases efficiency.

Employees need to seek continual improvement in best practices. Poor communication results in decreased innovation, hindering a company's long-term growth, and the ability to compete in an ever-changing global market.

When employees are intimidated by prior instances of emotionally charged negative communication, they may be unwilling to ask for clarification when provided with unclear directions. Unclear directions may be verbal or written, but neither of the formats is less intimidating to an employee who has been berated for prior mistakes.

Triangulation

According to Wayne Rivers, co-founder and president of the Family Business Institute, three forms of miscommunication haunt family-owned businesses:

Indirect communication happens when family members that work for the business discuss business matters with family members that do not work for the business. Healthy communicators speak directly to the person that needs to receive the message.

Triangulation occurs when a third party receives and redelivers the messages.

Meaningful triangulation is as simple as it sounds – triangulation without ill will. For example, an employee may have a fear of another employee's reaction to communication, based upon prior responses. Within that dysfunctional environment, the employee discusses an issue with a third party rather than directly with the person who lacks communication skills. This communication pattern remains dysfunctional but is practiced by those who are unable to communicate healthfully in a toxic environment.

Ill-intentioned triangulation is a game played by communication manipulators to draw others into the web of their toxic schemes. This communication pattern is dysfunctional and the manipulator gains gratification from introducing confusion and diverting attention from real issues. Negative communication continues, and solutions to business issues remain unsolved.

Triangulation can be minimized by both employees who refuse to discuss issues with triangulators, as well as by refusing to convey information received from a triangulator to the person for whom the message is intended. Simply put: never pass along information to a third party, or give the impression that it will be passed along.

All communication should be honest and allow for vulnerability.

According to the Light's Blog at lightshouse.org, communication in the family-owned business requires vulnerability. Individuals are unlikely to express their feelings and desires when their previous requests have been met with negativity and unproductive dialogue.

Family members should feel confident that expressing their desires will result in being heard, understood, and valued. Healthy communication in the family results in healing for the business, and the healing starts with honest and open communication. By addressing emotionally charged and offensive topics, individuals stop avoidance and silence in their tracks.

When addressing such topics, each member of the conversation should listen to the other without judgment. Discussions should not resort to interruption and belittling, whether verbal or non-verbal. Vocal tones should remain civil and pleasant, and facial expressions should remain neutral. Individuals should attempt to hear and understand each other and then work toward a mutually beneficial solution.

Family business experts concede that family ownership does have its privileges. But you have to intentionally run the business in a way that is fair, transparent and doesn't hurt the company morale, according to *7 Rules for Avoiding Conflicts of Interest in a Family Business* by Carolyn M. Brown.

Scripture Reference:

The Importance of True Unity

> *"Just as a body, though one, has many parts, but all its*
> *many parts form one body, so it is with Christ.*
> *- . (1 Corinthians 12:12 (NIV))"*

Chapter 3

CONFLICT RESOLUTION & DISAGREEMENTS

"Conflict cannot survive without your participation."
- Dr. Wayne Dyer

Scripture Reference

Love is patient and kind; love does not envy or boast; it is not arrogant.
- 1 Corinthians 13:4 (ESV)

Lack of boundaries may be demonstrated in some family-owned businesses. An employee/family member may be rude in her home life. Family members may tolerate it in that setting, accepting that this is the way she communicates. But conflicts in the workplace may boil over if the same behavior is allowed in the professional setting. People who exhibit rude behavior view life from the perspective of what is best for them, which can compromise the ability to reach resolutions around disagreements. This type of authoritative rule is not productive.

This presents a greater challenge in a family-owned business because there is no proper and established mechanism to resolve conflicts. In seeking to preserve the familial relationship, many will simply leave the family business.

We are all human beings who share varying opinions based on our life experiences. When these differences are embraced and accepted, we can discuss our different opinions and come up with meaningful, solution-oriented outcomes, focused on the best outcome for the business rather than individual agendas.

Sometimes in family-owned businesses, conflict shifts the focus away from the vision. If unchecked, the situation can devolve into a dysfunctional power struggle or manipulation to engineer an outcome that serves one individual's emotional needs, not the best interests of the business. This is worsened when family roles are involved and a level of disrespect and rudeness is rampant.

Systems can help because they create a level of transparency that will expose and limit people who control through manipulation. They will push back against the development of systems that will serve to expose their often secretive activities. Many times, this is the case in authoritative rule forms of management. If that is the management style you use, the goal of this section is simply to inform you of what to look out for when making decisions. It is not to change individual behavior. If the behavior does change, wonderful; but even if it does not, you are empowered in your decision making.

We cannot assume that all people are rational; many times, they are not, and they are putting your investment and livelihood on the line. It is best to know earlier on, so you have to make proper decisions. Also, do not assume that everyone wants to resolve conflict; some people benefit when dysfunction is created.

If the family-owned business lacks a clear and transparent system for addressing and solving conflicts, family members who are considering joining the business should carefully weigh the pros and cons. They should recognize that conflicts are likely to be both intensified and prolonged.

Some people just want a family-owned business to have their own chiefdom – not to support, grow, and promote others and the business. This is why it is so important that those in a family-owned business or thinking of joining one understand what they are dealing with before investing their time and energy.

Other people are conflict instigators who do not understand how to operate without conflict, so they create it everywhere they go. This is counterproductive to a successful business enterprise and compromises the interests of everyone involved. Those affected by a conflict instigator may feel that they are putting their energy into something that they know will not grow because of the inherent drama created by such people. This is especially crippling when the instigator happens to be in a leadership position or is the founder of the business.

The best way to deal with this issue is to have a system in place to resolve conflicts.

The ability to resolve conflict is key to the creation of a productive and sustainable work environment in which people feel safe, valued, and motivated. The inability to resolve conflict in meaningful and productive ways creates dysfunction and engenders communication paralysis. This is especially heightened in family-owned businesses due to personality conflicts and role intrusion.

Some family-owned businesses may operate autocratically, which creates issues because one individual controls all decisions with little input from group members. An autocrat's business decisions are based on their own ideas and judgment, and they rarely accept advice. This style of leadership is only effective when decisions are made quickly without consulting the larger group. However, this leadership style is most often problematic and results in a lack of creative solutions to problems, which ultimately hurts the business. This is relevant to conflict resolution because effective conflict resolution is usually not embraced by autocratic leaders, who are generally closed to ideas that challenge their leadership style.

Disagreements are merely differences of opinion, and they do not have to escalate into conflict. Most people who run a family-owned business do not have the skillset or personality to adequately resolve conflict. According to the Centre for Conflict Resolution, more than 65% of performance problems at work stem from strained workplace relationships, which result in decreased productivity, employee turnover, divided teams, poorly reflected management, and unhealthy confrontations.

This is especially true when the leader is unable to compromise or listen to ideas or he/she is defensive, combative, and emotionally driven. Rather than seeking resolution, these types of personalities must prove they are "right," and someone else is "wrong." In executing this strategy, all the workplace energy is focused on this flawed approach to conflict resolution. Resolution in these cases only results from getting what they desire, even though that is not in alignment with the growth or sustainability of the business.

Workplace conflict is more effectively addressed when mediated by an objective third party who is completely independent of the organizational structure. According to "Managing Conflict on the Farm" by Guy Hutt and Robert Milligan, there are six steps that help a family-owned business resolve conflict:

- <u>To initiate dialogue</u>, set a meeting with guidelines requiring everyone to listen to each other, speak honestly and respectfully, and only discuss one issue at a time.
- <u>Involving all parties</u> means that all team/family members are required to participate.
- <u>Assimilate information</u> during the first two steps by considering everyone's feelings, discussing the facts, and asking for clarification of unclear issues.
- <u>Reinforce agreements</u> of issues discussed, thereby building mutual trust and setting the stage for negotiation.
- <u>Negotiate disagreements</u> encountered during the discussion by outlining the issues and revisiting them with the intention of clarifying and understanding. Solve easier disagreements first, then tackle the more difficult ones. Work to bring the team to full agreement.
- <u>Finally, solidify agreements</u> by reviewing the discussion findings and creating commitment through verbal or written contracts.

Identifying the cause of the conflict is also important in family-owned businesses because the cause is more likely linked to some past family issues which have nothing to do with the business. It is critical to accept that many issues are based on the past. With this understanding, you can access professional tools to help navigate the process.

Some people are unable or unwilling to adequately engage in conflict resolution. So, it is important to decide if the working relationship is healthy for all involved. Sometimes a decision needs to be reached as to whether the business is right for each individual. If some people within the business are unwilling to adapt to progressive strategies to resolve conflicts, it must be recognized that they may not be able to successfully contribute to the family business.

Seeking assistance from outside the business is a great option. However, in many family-owned businesses, there is one person who makes the decisions. If this decision maker is resistant to change, this will create an obstacle for effective conflict resolution. Understanding this roadblock will help everyone make informed decisions. Some reasons people do not want to engage in effective conflict resolution include:

- conflict is often used as a tool for division and control
- conflict creates confusion
- narcissism in leadership, which leads to an inability to accept criticism

Therefore, no one person should be responsible for making all leadership decisions. Often, these people do not have the tools to make decisions that effectively empower the entire company. Checks and balances are also very important.

Engaging in conflict resolution requires respect, space for and value of different opinions, engagement, and involvement of others outside of the family system. Management training in conflict resolution should be mandatory, and participation of consultants in leadership decision-making can also be helpful. Unfortunately, both tools can be a barrier for leaders who are resistant to effective conflict resolution.

"The words of the tongue should have three gatekeepers:
It is true? Is it kind? Is it necessary?"

Arab Proverb

Chapter 4

RECOGNITION FOR STAFF EMPOWERMENT- INTERPERSONAL AND BUSINESS DEVELOPMENT

"Research indicates that workers have three primary needs: interesting work, recognition for doing a good job, and being let in on things that are going on in the company."
- Zig Ziglar

Scripture Reference

Therefore [a]comfort each other and [b]edify one another, just as you also are doing.
- 1 Thessalonians 5:11 (NKJV)

One of the most fundamental areas in which many family-owned businesses fall short is recognizing and appreciating staff. One of the core principles in human motivation is the need to be recognized and appreciated for our efforts. This is especially important in the family-owned business.

Corporations understand the benefits of basic recognition and often have standardized recognition programs. By contrast, many family-owned businesses feel that mentioning "good job," or receiving praise from a spouse or parent should be enough. However, this is not enough to encourage healthy growth and development for the individual and the business in return.

Businesses should use established appreciation and reward systems in which people have opportunities to work toward the fulfillment of defined goals to help inspire and motivate. In family-owned businesses, senior staff may arbitrarily distribute "rewards" based on how they feel, not in terms of the true benefits the staff provides to the company. They often do not see the value in a formal reward system. However, in most cases, the senior staff generally derives benefits from being "the bosses," such as opportunities for additional contracts, industry trade group participation, or other ancillary positions (ex., Board of Director positions). The business suffers if it lacks the proper rewards systems for junior staff.

Many who join family-owned businesses take on a great deal of responsibility yet do not have the same opportunities to benefit from the business as a senior member. Time may not allow them to be away from the business as they are busy doing their duties within the business. Additional time managing dysfunction often depletes productivity. Therefore, external recognition will not come in the same ways, which is why it is more important to reward them internally.

In *Synchronicity: The Inner Path of Leadership* (1996), Joseph Jaworski describes not only his father's experience in the Army but also his father's experiences as a prosecuting attorney for the Nuremberg and Watergate trials. Jaworski laments that his father never expressed his love, and while he believed his father loved him, he asked his father why it was never verbalized. His father confirmed that he did, and in fact does, love his son. Jaworski then expresses that it hurt him deeply to never hear the words.

The concept is much the same in family-owned businesses. Family members/employees assume that they are loved and respected, but these emotions need to be validated. Some families have a challenging time expressing emotion. In a family-owned business, owners and employees cannot take it for granted that everyone feels valued and appreciated. Love and recognition need to be expressed, and those feelings will equate to a healthy emotional and financial bottom line.

Employees receive external motivation when they receive recognition. They can couple the external motivation with their internal motivation and perform at higher levels. Gone are the days when family-owned businesses could rely on the adage "at least they have a job" to sustain employee/family members. If they are to thrive, employees need opportunities for innovation, as well as the building of self-esteem through positive feedback and feelings of success.

Appreciation and Rewards Systems

Be joyful always; pray continually; give thanks in all
circumstances; this is the will of God for your life.
- I Thessalonians 5:16 (NIV)

Generally, there is no system in place within family businesses to internally motivate, encourage, and support productive behaviors. Also, they usually lack a system for acknowledging the work of non-family staff at any level. The typical attitude that one should be happy simply because they have a job plagues beleaguered workers in a family-owned business and often causes undue stress, mismanagement, and fatigue. This is especially true in situations in which leadership lacks the motivation to find ways to properly motivate staff.

There always seems to be something more important or urgent that supersedes plans for employee recognition and other helpful initiatives. However, the fuel of any business is its people and if they are not motivated, energized, inspired and supported, the business will suffer. This is the plight of many family-owned businesses, and this issue tends to demoralize staff, both family members and non-family. A business that lacks employee recognition or incentives fails to build a culture that engenders concern for individual growth and development, which is required to foster company growth.

I have witnessed many second-generation family-owned business members relegated to work in the business with limited opportunities for building and fostering outside relationships because of internal inefficiencies. There is a lack of consideration on how junior staff can build fruitful external relationships because the senior members have reserved all of those opportunities for themselves. This has to be addressed in the work patterns and habits of the family-owned business members.

There are also no established procedures to celebrate successes or to acknowledge novel and innovative ideas. This leads to burnout, feelings of not being appreciated and questions of "Why am I here?" and "What are we doing?" A job must be more than just a paycheck.

People employed in the family business often spend far too many hours at work and, when away from the business physically, too many hours still focused on issues confronting the business. Too much energy flows in this direction, which can be draining. Attention is not given to creating an exciting environment in which contributions are acknowledged and appreciated, creating enthusiasm.

Family-owned businesses need to understand the importance of incorporating established appreciation and awards systems, in which all staff members' birthdays are celebrated and all relevant holidays are acknowledged with workplace decorations, etc. Monthly goals or challenges should be established, and those who meet these goals should be rewarded.

Moreover, staff members should be acknowledged for their contributions to the advancement of the business, including creating business partnerships, bringing new ideas, and creating new processes or procedures that increase efficiency. There should also be quarterly and annual appreciation goals established at the commencement of each year and fully shared with all staff to motivate participation. The contributions of individuals whose roles were essential in developing the business are often overlooked, especially when they are spouses or offspring of the "owners."

People are the currency of family business; the business could not have been built without the family commitment. That commitment is just as valuable as monetary investments.

The family business models that work best follow a common pattern: all parties involved have the quality of life they desire, with opportunities to pursue their own independent dreams/goals, while also being excited about what they contribute to the family business because they gain both financial and emotional rewards from the results of every effort. They are better contributors to the business because they bring to the table experience and knowledge gained through their independent ventures.

"Appreciate everything your associates do for the business. Nothing
else can quite substitute for a few well-chosen, well-timed, sincere
words of praise. They're absolutely free and worth a fortune."
- Sam Walton

Chapter 5

INDIVIDUAL GROWTH/ PERSONAL DEVELOPMENT

*"The strength of the team is each individual member.
The strength of each member is the team."*

- Phil Jackson

Scripture Reference

I can do all things through Christ who strengthens me.

- Philippians 4:13 (NKJV)

Faith without works is dead.

- James 2:26 (KJV)

Many fledging family-operated businesses do not demonstrate that they understand the importance of individual growth and development to the success of the business. However, for a business to grow and succeed, people must have a stake in the success of the business. For many, the opportunity to grow is a key part of being involved with an enterprise.

The need for growth aligns perfectly with human nature. People generally want to be a part of something outside of themselves that makes them feel good about themselves and their contributions. We spend many hours at the workplace, and a job is more than just a paycheck. Rather, it reflects how we feel about what we are producing. Meeting our basic needs is a critical component of job satisfaction and success.

If any business intends to thrive, its leadership must proactively invest in and support the growth and development of the company's most important asset: its people.

Many employees at family-owned businesses become so absorbed with day-to-day work duties that their capabilities may be managed but not developed for optimal output. This compromises productivity and assures that dynamic growth does not occur.

People are at their most enthusiastic and energetic when they believe in something and when they see how they are growing and learning from the experience in which they are participating, in this case, their job. In many family-owned businesses, individual growth is not supported. Due to the nature of the business, the roles of employees grow to meet the demands of the business. However, the growth in employees' roles is often for the sole benefit of the business and out of alignment with any meaningful personal growth for the employee. People end up working in the business, not on the business, and the business suffers.

Also, encouragement and planning for continuing education and training is typically not supported. Generally, there is no plan for current and future growth, and all decisions tend to be on the current "project" of the day.

It is important to have defined personal development support plans that encourage growth. This information needs to be integrated into the goals and objectives for all staff members, and the expectation that each staff member continues to learn and expand should be communicated. The business should make books, classes and other resources available, and should require staff to take maximum advantage of these educational opportunities.

According to Dan Millman, author of *The Four Purposes of Life: Finding Meaning and Direction in a Changing World*, there exists a "trinity of needs" when employees make a career choice. An employee may stay at a company when two of the three attributes exist, but all three are required for a long-term career investment:

- Does the company provide a useful service?
- Is the work personally satisfying?
- Can I thrive financially?

When an employee works at a company that provides these satisfying factors, a personal development plan for success can be implemented. The goal of such a plan is for individuals to grow in ways that complement their desires and skillsets. Businesses grow when employees grow. Companies benefit from innovative thinking and improved processes.

Training is an integral part of a personal development plan. Training on the company's vision and mission is an excellent start to ensure an employee's success whether new on the job or aspiring for a promotion.

In many businesses, whether family-owned or corporate; promotions to management positions are made within the company. Good managers provide direction and motivation within a team, yet family-owned businesses generally experience a lack of solid leadership. A popular saying is that people don't leave companies; they leave managers. To retain family members and employees, managers need training so that they do not undermine the growth and success of the company. The manager should focus on building employee strengths rather than his or her own.

Employment in the family-owned business should never be based on nepotism and entitlement. Rather, it should be a result of hard work, merit, and integrity. Staff should be supported with adequate training and quality coaching. This ensures that plans for succession are adequate. One tip is to pursue training specific to the company's industry. Managers should take courses on emotional intelligence to learn how to separate emotion from daily activities.

Mentoring

Benefits to the Employee

An employee benefits from a mentoring relationship because it provides him with someone with greater knowledge and experience to turn to for advice. While a mentor will not do the employee's job for him, the mentor may demonstrate a task, guide the employee through solving a problem or critique the employee's work.

A mentorship may help an employee feel less isolated at work and encourage him to interact more with others. A mentor can provide an employee with tips on career growth and introduce the employee to other professionals. As the employee matures in his career, a mentor may remain a valued adviser to the employee.

Benefits to the Employer

The employer of a mentored employee gains from greater productivity in the workplace. As employees turn to their mentors for advice, they make fewer mistakes on the job, cutting losses to the employer. Employees in mentoring relationships tend to have greater job satisfaction as well, which can mean a more positive work environment. Employers might also notice less turnover of employees as workers feel greater loyalty to the company. A company might even use its mentoring program to attract new employees.

Benefits to the Profession

Mentoring in the workplace can have long-term benefits as employees become more self-directed and develop stronger communication and problem-solving skills. This allows a business to become more creative and focus its attention on growth, rather than training. Mentored employees value collaboration and sharing of information, which can lead to a stronger organization. Mentored workers are also apt to become involved in professional organizations that further both their careers and the profession itself.

Staff Development Opportunities

External input/training for staff and management should be continuously required. Family-owned businesses tend to function in a vacuum, which produces creative voids and stifles the infusion of new trends and ideas. Requiring staff to consistently participate in training outside of the business fosters a sense of responsibility and personal growth. It also brings much-needed information into the business. Also, retreats and team-building exercises help keep all staff engaged, informed, and involved.

> *"Outstanding leaders go out of their way to boost the self-esteem of their personnel;*
> *if people believe in themselves, it's amazing what they can accomplish."*
>
> *- Sam Walton*

Chapter 6

FORECASTING, VALUE AND EQUITABLE INCOME DISTRIBUTION

"A man who does not plan long ahead will find trouble at this door."
- Confucius

Scripture Reference

A good person leaves an inheritance for their children's children,
but a sinner's wealth is stored up for the righteous..
-Proverbs 13:22 (NIV)

Anyone entering a professional work environment expects and is entitled to an effective and transparent plan for growth. If that growth plan is not forthcoming, that employee becomes empowered to seek other employment options that are aligned with their individual expectations and goals. However, in family-owned businesses, one of two things often occur: either the owner/founder makes unsupported promises of growth opportunities that never materialize and rebuffs conversations when addressed after employment is confirmed, or the issue is never discussed nor considered. Both scenarios create a major void and lead to staff dissatisfaction, thereby negatively impacting the overall business.

With the intertwining that inherently exists among individuals within the business, it also is fair to assume that positive actions taken by one benefits the whole. Actions that are less than optimal, unfair, misleading, or not transparent have a negative impact on the entire organization. Therefore, the ability to effectively forecast one's individual and collective goals is based on the family-owned business' ability to understand the importance of developing and adhering to policies in which the decision-making environment is not arbitrary and unilateral.

Often, the business' management will lead staff on with the promise of long-term growth opportunities, but more often than not, these are never realized. Often these promises are only used to manipulate people and keep them engaged, involved, and giving their best work while their career potential stagnates. Since the opportunities and goals for growth are never documented, there is no transparency and no foundation upon which to rely for current or future growth. This compromises the business for all, most frequently as the result of a decision executed by one.

In family-owned businesses, the determination of salary ranges is usually not based on performance or reviewed for market competitiveness. There is often no action regarding retirement funding/planning, no long-term incentives for income growth, no pattern of growth and no shared wealth building. Setting and reviewing achievable goals tied to income is often non-existent. Therefore, the staff operates at the pleasure of the major decision-maker who, in many cases, imposes heavy time demands on staff due to poor planning and ineffective implementation of operational systems meant to streamline the business. This can result in many wasted hours during the workday, evenings and weekends, as well as ineffectiveness in problem-solving, troubleshooting and dealing with crises. This all results from having no plan for the short or long-term future. Employees are not looking for assurances or guarantees, but a general idea of what they can expect in income growth and opportunity expansion.

The major decision-maker often expects employees to be excited and encouraged when the business makes revenue. However, those who helped build the business are often not fairly compensated for their efforts. Most people do not work for a family-owned business solely for a paycheck, so the fact that they "have a job" is not enough. Remember, they got involved in the business to help and support its growth, even when the company could not attract and hire dedicated external staff to support the business' operations and growth. This diminishes the incentive for people to want to be invested in the business as it negatively impacts morale and leads to increased turnover for non-family staff. Even those who remain in the business become less than committed. They have no idea what they are committed to.

Moreover, when there is no effective communication and no transparent, objective and democratic method in place for forecasting, the result is a lack of long-term viability for the business. It is reflected in the lack of quality in many of the family-owned businesses that survive. Those businesses that grow have systems in place that address individual needs to plan their course by providing support for the basic needs of anyone involved in the business.

The fundamental issue here is an overall lack of appreciation and respect for what others bring to the company. This lack is demonstrated when the company fails to support individual growth and future planning. The key is to identify what the issues are so that employees can make appropriate decisions for themselves.

Benefits/Retirement Planning

Provisions for retirement and other benefits are almost always overlooked in family-owned businesses, which creates a void that causes second-generation "owners" to leave in order to gain control over these important elements. Since pay grades in family-owned businesses are not typically commensurate with income for competing responsibilities and roles in the broader market, it is often more attractive for the second generation to seek more stable situations in which they are assured some growth.

Business Planning

Advanced planning that is communicated to all staff is important for stability, transparency, motivation and morale. Many businesses, however, do not have a formal annual planning process. This leads to uncertainty and insecurity. All staff must be aware of the plans for the business so that they can focus on their day-to-day tasks without unnecessarily dwelling on the unknown.

The ability to plan is strongly connected to one's career path. In a family-owned business, an individual's career path is generally unclear, haphazard, and informal. The ability to have a goal, articulate a vision and take the necessary daily steps to achieve it is compromised if individual and company forecasting is not addressed. Value in the workplace is derived in part by one's contribution, acknowledgement of that contribution, and compensation reflective of the contributions rendered.

We have previously discussed that acknowledgement of professional and personal achievement is inadequately addressed in most family-owned businesses. Monetary compensation is another way to acknowledge an employee's contributions to the business. Unfortunately, in many family-owned businesses, compensation is not equitably distributed, nor is there a clear and transparent compensation plan. As a result, staff members sometimes work for years in the business and yet, despite business growth, they see no increase in income. However, when business is slow, there is inevitably a direct impact on personal income.

The incentive to help build the business to be more profitable is compromised since there is no vested interest in doing so. Often, when revenue does increase again, staff members still do not directly benefit from income growth. Decision-makers often contend that the increase is used to support business operations. Therefore, the staff should feel lucky to have the jobs that are provided by the business' continuing operations. However, such shallow thinking is short-sighted and stifles participation, involvement, innovation and growth. In most professional organizations and businesses that believe in providing an atmosphere of growth, there is a keen awareness that the growth of the individual leads to the growth of the company.

It is important to utilize forecasting tools. This encourages involvement, innovation and interaction while also providing the necessary transparency for good decision-making. It helps the business determine if it is really interested in forging a path of new ideas or if it is staying on a path where new ideas are not supported.

There is power in transparency. It levels the playing field and prevents staff from being strung along for years. It reveals whether company leadership intends to fully embrace new and innovative ideas or allow for growth opportunities both professionally and personally.

The ability to effectively plan for life is inherently connected with the work one does. Effective forecast planning, however, is often compromised or not even considered in the operations of many family-owned businesses. Typically, the decision-maker in a family-owned business presumes to intuit the life plans of all, especially family members who join the business.

This decision-maker often falls into the role of either doling out money upon request or unilaterally devising a way to integrate others into the family business without consideration of the individual's personal goals and objectives.

The business owner/founder may induce hiring with promises of growth, then not deliver the resources needed to attain that growth. In that circumstance, the family staff person remains frozen at the same wage level. New ideas are integrated, and responsibilities are increased, but there is no corresponding increase in salary or management control of the project. This stifles creativity and increases job dissatisfaction.

The bottom line is that the staff is left at a disadvantage and waiting for the decision-maker to implement new plans and ideas, which often never come to life. Innovation is fostered by new and emergent ideas and by young thinkers and doers. Without this energy, the business remains stagnant, and no real, sustainable growth occurs. This is another reason why talent often leaves family-owned businesses. Staff decisions and innovative ideas are not supported and cannot be developed.

Since much is intertwined in family-owned businesses, one can see how this issue can present problems with sustainability. Only 25% of family-owned businesses survive, and this issue is the primary cause of failure for many of them. Critical intervention is necessary to both bring this issue to light and address the topic.

Generally, senior leaders at family-owned businesses find comfort in the status quo and are often intimidated by new ideas that they cannot fully understand. This creates resistance, and instead of looking for solutions, learning about new ideas and considering industry advances, artificial barriers are placed around the issue, or false promises are given to consider ideas later. All the while, the intention is never legitimate, innovation is stifled, growth is thwarted, and opportunities for professional and personal growth are greatly diminished.

> *"To work for salary is to mortgage your life."*
>
> *- Sunday Adelaya*

Conclusion

Just because that's where you started doesn't mean that's where you are meant to end up.

You can't properly prepare for your future and set your family up for success if you remain crippled by lack of information.

Business is about growth. It's not about the growth of just one person or one generation, but rather it's about building upon each generation, so the next generation is not starting from scratch. It's about leaving a legacy in which individual contributions are seen for generations to come because that is the overall intention and vision. It is a fruitless effort to continue to invest in something that is dying because it is in a strangle-hold of dysfunction. It is better not to contribute at all. It's best to plow your resources, energy and creativity into something that has sustainable growth.

In conclusion, what I have learned is that it is best to enter into any relationship with a vision of where you want to end up and how you want the results of your efforts to manifest. Also, seek things that are of great importance to you and align with it. Early identification of issues or unhelpful patterns which may impair your growth or the business success will allow you to make informed decisions.

Know that conforming to dysfunction is never normal. Align yourself with the clarity of your spirit – it speaks to you in subtle ways to let you know if something is not right, even if you can't identify the "something" specifically. Surround yourself with positive people who share your moral fiber and vision. Align with people whose words reflect their actions, align with people who encourage you to go higher, not for their gain, but because it's what's best for you. Align yourself with people you feel good being around and whose energy is uplifting. Begin your journey, follow your heart, and your feet will know the way!

"For I know the plans I have for you," declares the LORD, "plans to prosper you and not to harm you, plans to give you hope and a future."

Jeremiah 29:11 (NIV)

References

Assertiveness and the Four Styles of Communication. (n.d.). Retrieved from

http://serenityonlinetherapy.com/assertiveness.htm

Bork, D. (2009, November 18). Maintaining Relationships – The 5th Key to Success in Family Business. Retrieved from

https://www.familybusinessmatters.consulting/maintaining-relationships-the-5th-key-to-success-in-family-business/

Celebrating Achievement: Recognize Success to Increase Motivation. (n.d.). Retrieved from

https://www.mindtools.com/pages/article/celebrating-achievement.htm

Faris, S. (2019, March 12). Effects of Negative Communication in the Workplace. Retrieved from

http://smallbusiness.chron.com/effects-negative-communication-workplace-11524.html

Hofstrand, D. (n.d.). Resolving Family and Business Conflicts.

https://www.extension.iastate.edu/agdm/wholefarm/html/c4-74.html

Hutt, G., Milligan, R. "Managing Conflict on the Farm." (n.d.). Retrieved from https://core.ac.uk/download/pdf/159556728.pdf

Indalecio, T. (2019, January 24). 5 Common Threats to a Family Business. Retrieved from https://www.thebalancesmb.com/threats-to-family-business-1240718

Light's Blog A Blog About Toxic and Non-Toxic People. (n.d.).

http://lightshouse.org/lights-blog/psychological-triangulation#axzz3MGmrzKTh

Mallinger, M., Goodwin, D., O'Hara, T. (2009). Recognizing Organizational Culture in Managing Change. Retrieved from

http://gbr.pepperdine.edu/2010/08/recognizing-organizational-culture-in-managing-change/

Millman, D. (2001). The Four Purposes of Life: Finding Meaning and Direction in a Changing World. HJ Kramer/New World Library.

Odine, M. Communication Problems in Management. (2015). *Journal of Emerging Issues in Economics, Finance and Banking, 4* (2), 1615 – 1630. http://globalbizresearch.org/economics/images/files/54946_ID_S528_JEIEFB_Maurice%20Odine.pdf

Stalk, G., Foley H. (January 2012). Avoid the Traps That Can Destroy Family Businesses. Retrieved from https://hbr.org/2012/01/avoid-the-traps-that-can-destroy-family-businesses

Swart, G. (2013, June 8). 7 Ways to Build and Retain a Strong Team as Your Company Grows. Retrieved from

https://thenextweb.com/insider/2013/06/08/7-ways-to-build-and-retain-a-strong-team-as-your-company-grows/